GW01464282

TWO BEARS

and the fireworks

Story by Cathie and David Bell

Pictures by Jan Brychta

Oxford University Press

For Emily

Oxford University Press, Walton Street, Oxford OX2 6DP

Oxford   New York   Toronto
Delhi   Bombay   Calcutta   Madras   Karachi
Petaling Jaya   Singapore   Hong Kong   Tokyo
Nairobi   Dar es Salaam   Cape Town
Melbourne   Auckland

and associated companies in
Berlin   Ibadan

Oxford is a trade mark of Oxford University Press

© Oxford University Press 1990
Printed in Hong Kong

A CIP catalogue record for this book is available from the
British Library.

The Two Bears Books are:

Two Bears at the seaside
Two Bears in the snow
Two Bears at the party
Two Bears go fishing
Two Bears find a pet
Two Bears and the fireworks

Winston opened a letter.
It said 'Please come to my fireworks party tonight.
Love from Sam.'

Stanley wasn't very happy about the fireworks.
'I don't like big bangs,' he said.
'Don't worry,' said Winston. 'You can wear my ear muffs.'

That night, they dressed up in very warm clothes.
Winston was excited. Stanley wore the ear muffs,
but he still wasn't very happy.

On the way to the party, the bears passed some
children.
They knocked Stanley over!
They had boxes of fireworks in their hands.
'Let's go to the woods!' shouted one of them.

When the bears arrived at the party, all the
children were crying.
'What's happened?' said Winston.
'The fireworks have been stolen,' said Sam's dad.

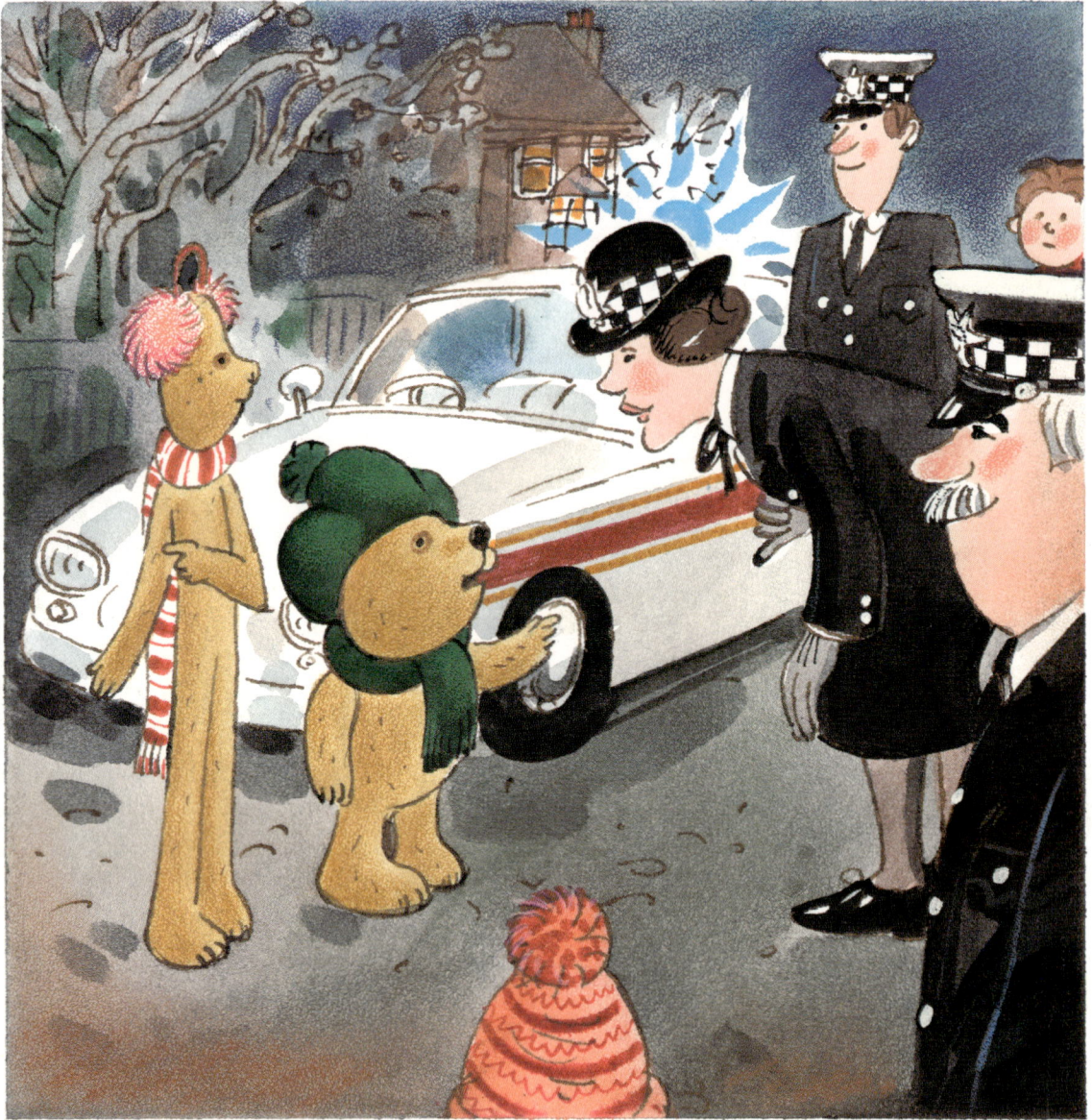

The police arrived.
'I know who stole the fireworks!' said Winston.
'And I know where they are!' said Stanley.
'Come with us!' shouted the police.

The police cars raced along the road with their blue
lights flashing.

When the gang saw the police cars they dropped the
fireworks and tried to run away.
The police jumped out.
They ran after the gang and caught them.

Winston and Stanley picked up the fireworks.
There were still lots left to take back to the party.

The police took the gang away in one car.
Then they put all the fireworks in the other car,
and drove the bears back to the party.

The children cheered when they saw the two bears
with the fireworks.

Sam's dad looked in the boxes.
'All the bangers have gone,' he said.
'I'm glad,' said Stanley. 'I hate bangers.'

Stanley took off his ear muffs and watched the fireworks.
There were rockets, catherine wheels, and sparklers.
Everyone had a wonderful time.

Sam's dad brought out sausages and baked
beans for everyone.
'I'm glad the gang didn't steal these bangers,' laughed
Winston.